Milo and the Robots

Written by Mary-Anne Creasy

Illustrated by Roberto Barrios Angelelli

Flying Start
to Literacy®

Contents

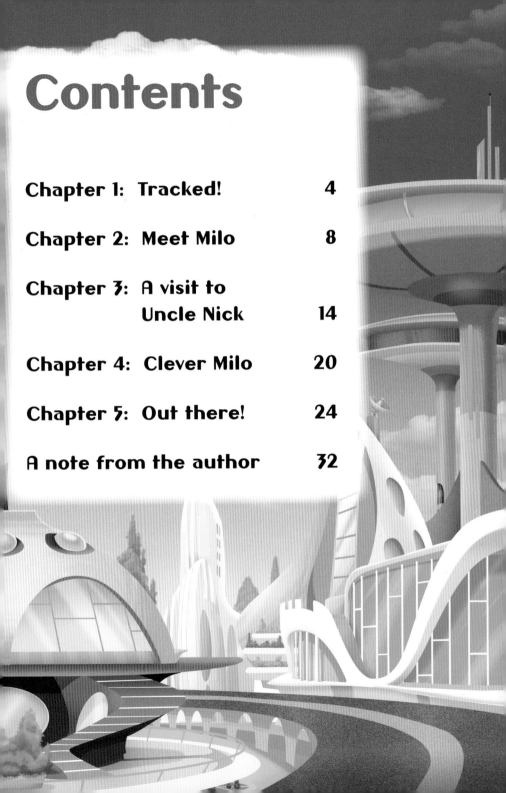

Chapter 1
Tracked!

Seb and Amy were late again.

"Oh no," said Amy. The hall monitor was scanning another student who was late for class.

"Quick, let's just sneak past," whispered Seb.

But of course you can't sneak past a robot.

"Stop, please!" said the hall monitor. A green light flashed on their faces – they had been identified.

"Seb and Amy Jones, you are late for the third time this week."

"But our mum didn't—" began Seb.

"Please extend your Tracklets."

They both held out their wrists, and then their Tracklets beeped.

"Now continue directly to class," said the hall monitor.

Class had already started. Seb and Amy scanned their Tracklets and sat down in front of their screens, then put on their headphones. Amy turned to wave to a friend.

"Amy Jones! Pay attention!" said a voice in her headphones. Amy jumped as the camera eye above her screen flashed in her eyes. There was no escaping the class monitor!

After school, Seb and Amy watched enviously as kids tapped their Tracklets onto E-Scoots and zoomed off.

"I asked Mum to refill our Tracklets last night," said Amy as they walked home. "She must have forgotten again."

"I think she's worried about Uncle Nick," said Seb.

"I know, it's so weird he left the city," said Amy. "I mean, who would want to live in the country? And without the latest robots!"

When they arrived home, they scanned their Tracklets and stood in front of the face scanner.

"Welcome home, Seb and Amy," said HOWY, their robot. "Your mother would like to talk to you."

Their mother's face appeared on a large screen in the living room.

"Why are you home so late?" asked Mum, looking worried.

"We didn't have any credit on our Tracklets, so we had to walk home from school," said Seb.

"Sorry, I forgot to refill them. But I have great news. Uncle Nick has sent a surprise for you, which should be arriving soon. He said you should open it very carefully and keep it inside the house until I get home."

"Okay!"

"Now, what's for dinner tonight, HOWY?" asked Mum. "Please scan fridge contents and plan this evening's meal."

HOWY pinged. "Confirmed. Lasagna and salad will be served at 6:30 this evening."

Then the screen flickered and Mum disappeared.

Chapter 2

Meet Milo

HOWY suddenly blared: "Delivery! Your parcel has now arrived."

Seb and Amy ran to the delivery chute. Inside was a box with holes.

"Wow, it's heavy," said Seb.

"Quick, open it!" said Amy excitedly.

Seb scanned his Tracklet on the lock and then the lid popped open. Inside, curled up asleep, was a small dog.

"Oh, it's so cute!" said Amy. "Mum must have told Uncle Nick how much I miss Bella."

"Its name is Milo," said Seb as he checked the tag on the puppy's collar. "But where are the instructions?"

Amy lifted it out. "Wow, it's really floppy. It must be one of the new-generation robo-pets," she said.

The puppy started to move. It stretched and yawned, then wagged its tail and barked.

"Let's sync it to HOWY so we can control it," said Seb.

"HOWY, sync Milo!" said Amy.

"Sorry, unable to detect device named Milo," said HOWY.

"HOWY, make Milo stop barking," said Amy.

"Sorry, unable to detect device named Milo," repeated HOWY.

"Let's put it back in the box until Mum gets home," said Seb.

But when Seb reached to pick up Milo, it bounced up onto the chair next to an open window and then jumped out the window before they could stop it.

"Quick, we have to catch it!" said Amy.

"HOWY, open door!" yelled Seb.

The door slid open, and Seb and Amy ran outside, frantically looking for the dog.

Milo was in the park, trying to play with another boy's dog. Milo was barking and wagging its tail.

"What's wrong with your dog?" asked the boy. "It's out of control."

The boy threw a ball and his dog ran to fetch it. Milo chased the ball too and caught it, and kept on running towards the pond in the middle of the park. Then it jumped straight in, splashing around happily. A group of ducks flew away, quacking with alarm. Seb and Amy ran over, panting.

"Is this your dog?" asked the police officer, after he got Milo out of the pond and attached a leash to its collar.

Amy nodded nervously. "Yes, sorry, we just got it and we couldn't sync it to our HOWY."

The police officer tried to scan Milo. "The device is defective. It is not scanning. I have to take it to the police station and destroy it!"

"No, please don't take it away!" said Amy.

"We'll take it home now, we promise," said Seb. "And we will return it to the manufacturer."

"Okay," said the police officer. "I will contact your mother to make sure you do."

Amy and Seb held out their wrists so their Tracklets could be scanned, and then they hurried back home with Milo.

"This is the surprise from Uncle Nick?" asked Mum, when Amy and Seb arrived home.

"Yes, it's our new robo-dog," said Seb.

"But there's something wrong with it," said Amy. "We can't sync it to HOWY. And it jumped out the window and got into lots of trouble!"

Mum picked up Milo, and it licked her face.

"Kids, this isn't a robo-dog – it's a real dog."

"What? A real live dog? You mean it's not a robot?"

"That's right, a real live dog. It's Uncle Nick's idea of a joke, I'm sure," said Mum, annoyed. "We have to send Milo back to Uncle Nick."

"Can't we keep it?" asked Seb. "We promise we'll look after it."

"Please, Mum. We want a real dog," said Amy.

Their mother shook her head. "I'm sorry, but no one has live pets anymore. They're too chaotic. We will have to send Milo back to Uncle Nick."

Amy and Seb knew their mother meant it – Milo had to go. Then Amy had a bright idea.

"Mum, maybe Seb and I could take Milo back to Uncle Nick. It's Saturday tomorrow, so we don't have school."

"We can make sure Milo doesn't get into trouble!" said Seb.

"Well, that's probably a good idea," said Mum. "I'll call Uncle Nick now."

Chapter 3

A visit to Uncle Nick

The following morning, Amy and Seb were up early. They had never been outside the city before and they couldn't wait to set off for Uncle Nick's place.

"The Go-Car will take you straight there," said Mum, as Amy, Seb and Milo jumped in the car.

The driverless car hovered quietly along the road, past the tall glass buildings and over the sky bridge. Soon they were far from the city. The road cut right through the middle of a large field of crops surrounded by a thick forest.

A light flashed on the control panel of the Go-Car. "Destination will be reached in approximately twenty minutes."

"Great, we're nearly there," said Amy as she patted Milo.

But then the Go-Car started to beep and slow down.

"Just go straight ahead," said Seb. "Please keep going."

"I'm sorry, I'm unable to navigate any further. The signal has been lost," said the Go-Car, as it slowed to a stop. "Please exit the vehicle."

"What do we do now?" asked Amy, looking worried.

"Let's contact Mum." Seb commanded his Tracklet: "Call Mum." But there was no response. "I don't understand – it says No Signal."

"It's not far to Uncle Nick's," said Amy. "Let's walk!"

Amy and Seb started down the long and empty road. It was so quiet. There were no sounds from cars, or scooters, or people talking or other sounds of the city. There was only the sound of their feet on the road and the breeze rustling the crops.

Suddenly, Milo seemed to get a scent of something and pulled the leash out of Seb's hand. Before they could do anything, Milo had disappeared through the tall crops, barking.

"Milo!" yelled Seb. "Come back!"

"Milo, stop!" shouted Amy.

They ran through the rows of crops, their feet sinking into the soft earth. They followed Milo further and further into the crops, but the dog's barking grew distant.

Amy and Seb slowed down. The crops were much thicker in the middle of the field and taller, too – taller than Seb and Amy. They could no longer see Milo's paw prints, nor could they hear the dog's barking.

"I can't even see the road," said Amy. "I don't even know which direction it is."

"Let's head for that forest. Maybe I can climb a tree and see where we are," said Seb.

"A tree? You've never climbed a tree. We're not allowed to climb them at home," said Amy.

"Well, I can try," said Seb, annoyed. "But we'd better hurry. The sun is getting low in the sky."

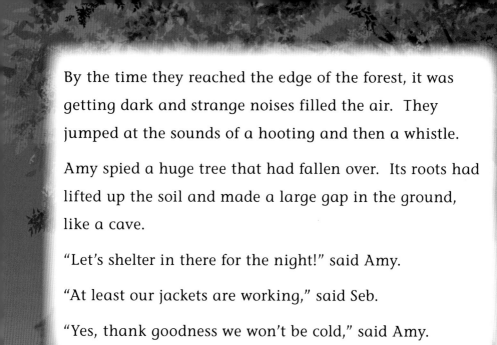

By the time they reached the edge of the forest, it was getting dark and strange noises filled the air. They jumped at the sounds of a hooting and then a whistle.

Amy spied a huge tree that had fallen over. Its roots had lifted up the soil and made a large gap in the ground, like a cave.

"Let's shelter in there for the night!" said Amy.

"At least our jackets are working," said Seb.

"Yes, thank goodness we won't be cold," said Amy.

Their mum had just bought each of them the latest jacket, which senses when the body is too cold or hot and adjusts its temperature accordingly.

"Are you okay?" asked Seb.

"Yeah, I'm thirsty, though," said Amy. "And hungry."

"We're just going to have to stay here till morning," said Seb. "Maybe they'll send someone to find us."

"But how?" asked Amy. "We're in the middle of a forest and no tracking device works out here."

Chapter 4

Clever Milo

"Shhh," said Amy. "What's that?"

They heard distant barking, then someone called out, "Amy! Seb!"

Suddenly, Milo was wriggling down into the cave, barking and licking them.

"Milo!" they yelled, hugging the small dog close. Then they scrambled out of their hiding space.

A figure appeared out of the darkness.

"Uncle Nick!" they called in relief, running to him.

"You found us!" said Amy, hugging him.

"Milo found you, actually," said Uncle Nick, reaching down to pat the dog. "This clever dog found its old home, then led me to you."

"Good boy, Milo!" They leant down to pat it.

"I called your mother to say you hadn't arrived yet, and then Milo showed up," said Uncle Nick. "Wow, you kids are a real mess. What happened? Did you get lost?"

As they walked to his house, they told Uncle Nick all about their adventure – the Go-Car losing its signal, the chase after Milo and getting lost.

When they finally got to Uncle Nick's, they were exhausted and could barely keep their eyes open.

"I thought you lived in a town," said Amy. "I can't see anything, it's so dark."

"It's a village, which is like a tiny town. Only about 50 people live here, but it's growing," said Uncle Nick.

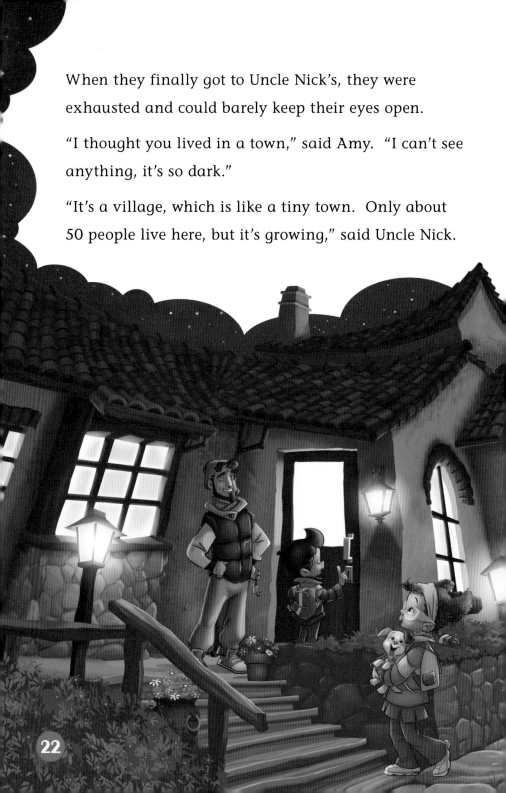

He opened a creaky gate and they walked up a path to a house they could see outlined in the moonlit sky. They staggered up the wooden stairs.

"Open door!" said Seb, but the door didn't open.

"I don't think your face scanner is working," said Amy.

Uncle Nick shook his head as he searched his pockets and pulled out a large key.

"I don't have a face scanner. We use the old-fashioned kind of security here!"

They followed Uncle Nick into the house, but were too exhausted and barely looked at their surroundings. The table was set for dinner, with bread and cheese and fruit.

"I'm starving," said Amy and Seb together.

As soon as they had eaten, they followed Uncle Nick through the house to a small room with two beds. They changed into their pyjamas and fell into a deep sleep.

Chapter 5
Out there!

In the morning, Amy and Seb awoke with a jerk. Milo jumped on their beds and licked their faces, barking at them.

Uncle Nick was standing at the open door. "How did you sleep, kids? I'm cooking breakfast, so wash up and get dressed. I called your mum and let her know you're okay. She's coming to get you later."

The kids washed up and then changed into their spare clothes from their backpacks. "Let's hurry, I'm starving," said Amy. "Something smells delicious."

They walked out and stepped into the large, simply furnished room. Nick was in the kitchen area, doing something strange. Seb and Amy watched him for a moment.

"What are you doing?" asked Amy.

"I'm cooking eggs," said Nick. "Anyone want toast?"

"Yes, please," said Seb. Loudly, he commanded, "HOWY, please make toast."

The kids looked around, waiting for HOWY to reply. Nick started laughing.

"There's no HOWY here, kids," he said. "You'll have to make it yourself."

"Wow, I've never seen these things before," said Amy.

"Most appliances you buy now are automatic and do what you ask them to. But those things don't work here, so we had to find old fridges and toasters and fix them up. We did it ourselves, here in the village," said Uncle Nick.

Milo followed Amy to the fridge. "Do you have any milk?" But the fridge didn't reply. "How do you know what's in the fridge?"

"You have to open it and look inside," said Uncle Nick.

Amy opened the fridge and peered inside, pushing things aside until she found the milk. "I think I like our system better. Where are the meal-processing packets?"

"I plan my meals, then I cook using the ingredients I already have," said Nick. "We even grow our own fruit and vegetables in the community garden. I never did these things when I lived in the city, but now I love looking after my house and cooking."

"Does everyone live like this out here?" asked Seb.

"Yes, there are no HOWYs, no robots, no E-Scoots, no Go-Cars. I moved here because I want to live outside the city, without all the technology," said Uncle Nick. "I still want *some* technology. I just don't want everything to be controlled by AI."

After breakfast, Uncle Nick showed them how to wash the dishes and then they vacuumed the floor.

"Let's go for a walk around the village," said Uncle Nick after they had finished all their chores.

They put Milo on the leash and walked down the road towards the village. It was strangely quiet. There were no E-Scoots, Go-Cars or flying cars. Kids were riding bikes or just walking. They weren't even looking at Tracklets.

At the grocery store, Uncle Nick took a basket and they filled it up. There were no machines roaming around and stacking shelves, only a man who asked them if he could help them find anything.

When they had finished shopping, they looked around for the machines to check them out. They came to the checkout and there was a girl there. She smiled and said, "Hi, Nick. How's it going?"

"Great," said Uncle Nick. "Meet Seb and Amy. They're visiting me from the city."

"How do you like it out here?" asked the girl.

Amy and Seb stammered as the girl scanned the items and bagged them.

"It's nice to chat to someone instead of dealing with a robot, isn't it?" said Uncle Nick as they left the store.

At the park, there was a fenced area. Inside were some kids with their dogs. They let Milo off the leash, and it ran up to the other dogs and they sniffed one another. Then Milo jumped up, put its muddy paws on one of the other kids and barked.

"We definitely need to train Milo," said Uncle Nick as Seb went over and dragged Milo away, apologising for the muddy marks on the other kid's clothes.

Nick showed them how to train Milo to come when called. He told Milo to sit, and then gave the dog a treat when it did.

Seb and Amy tried it, too. At first Milo just wanted to play and ignore their commands for it to come and sit. It was frustrating, but they kept at it all afternoon, and gradually, Milo learnt to come and to sit when called.

Then they heard someone yelling.

"Hey, Seb! Amy! Nick!"

It was Mum. She walked over, wearing a nice new pantsuit, waving at them.

Milo barked excitedly and ran towards her, its ears flopping and tongue lolling.

Mum's smile changed to a look of alarm.

The kids yelled, "Milo, stop – come back!"

But Milo kept running towards their mother.

Then Mum pointed to the ground and yelled, "Milo, sit!"

Milo skidded to a halt and sat obediently, wagging its tail.

Their mother bent over and patted the dog. "Good boy, Milo, good boy."

The kids came running over, looking anxiously at their mother as she hugged them.

"Sorry, Mum," said Seb. "We've been training it all afternoon."

"It's learning to be more obedient," said Amy. "Do you think we could keep Milo?"

Their mother smiled. "I think Milo would make a great pet for us," she said. "At least Milo listens to me!"

A note from the author

Technology, including robots, has made many everyday tasks easier and faster. One day soon, we might forget how to do some things.

I wondered what it might be like in a futuristic world where we have robot pets, instead of real ones. Would we know what to do? What if some kids were suddenly given a real dog – a dog that doesn't obey them like a robot? I also wanted to show that relying on technology for everything might not be such a good idea.